THE OLD HOME PLACE

Susan Dart

CHICAGO SPECTRUM PRESS

©1997 by Susan Dart

All rights reserved. Except for appropriate use in critical reviews or works of scholarship, the reproduction or use of this work in any form or by any electronic, mechanical, or other means now known or hereafter invented, including photocopying and recording, and in any information storage and retrieval system, is forbidden without written permission of the author.

CHICAGO SPECTRUM PRESS
4848 BROWNSBORO CENTER ARCADE
LOUISVILLE, KY 40207
1-800-594-5190

Printed in the U.S.A.

10 9 8 7 6 5 4 3 2 1

ISBN: 1-886094-52-7

For Jack and our three children,
Anne, Mary, and John

CONTENTS

CHAPTER ONE
    The House and the History   9

CHAPTER TWO
    The Johnson Years   19

CHAPTER THREE
    The Sherfy Years   35

CHAPTER FOUR
    The Garrett Years   43

CHAPTER FIVE
    The McCutcheon Years   69

    Family Trees   86
    Chronology   89
    Acknowledgments and
    Sources of Information   91
    Books and Publications   93
    Index   97

ONE

CHAPTER ONE

The House and the History

This is the story of a house and the people who lived in it. The old timers call it "the old home place." Some people call it the "old house," and sometimes, though erroneously, the "cabin"—erroneously because the word "cabin" connotes a rustic hut. In any case, the official name on the National Register of Historic Places is more pretentious than any of these. Traditionally historic houses are called by the name of the first owners, so it is officially the John Hiram Johnson House.

But John (or sometimes Johnny) Johnson, who actually built the house with his own hands, would have been astonished. He built it in 1887 for his bride to be, and it was just a house. It may have been a little finer, a little more carefully built, than most of the other houses in the neighborhood, but still it was just a plain, honest house. It had real windows with glass panes, to be sure—windows that went up and down—whereas most of the houses in the neighborhood had only crude openings for windows with nothing but single wooden shutters, hinged on the sides, to keep out the elements.

John Johnson's house also had two separate bedrooms in addition to the main room with the fireplace, and it was built inside and out with lumber from a sawmill instead of plain logs. But so were many—probably most—of the other houses nearby. Why then the fuss a century later? The main reason is that it's the only house anywhere around of its era that is still standing, intact and hardly changed, almost as it was over a hundred years ago. And it's never been modernized or moved. It's precisely where it's always been.

It's in the foothills of the Blue Ridge Mountains in Polk County, which is in the southwestern part of North Carolina. To get there you must go about five miles from the small town of Saluda down Holbert Cove Road, which threads its way through the mountains bordered by deep and dangerous drops to a creek far below. After a dozen scary hairpin curves, you come to a narrow winding driveway on your left, parts of which are only two ruts, the same two ruts that have always been there. The house is a half mile from Holbert Cove Road, at the top of a hill. Today it has a street address, 99 Holbert Cove Road, which is another thing that would have astonished John Johnson. Even in the late 1980s the assignment of street numbers to every house on that rustic, unpaved road was considered an unnecessary intrusion in the area.

When John Johnson built his house, there were not only no house numbers, there was no mail delivery on Holbert Cove Road. That came long after the Johnsons had moved away—1947, to be exact. Before that if you got a letter (not an everyday occurrence, in any case), you went to the Saluda post office on Main Street to pick it up.

A Little Historic Background

The first people in the area that we know anything about were the Cherokee Indians, who early on had achieved an advanced way of life. They lived in log houses, farmed the fertile land, and were a peaceful, civilized people. Then the white man arrived. As always—inevitably—there was trouble. There were clashes and as always—inevitably—the white man won out in the end. The chapter in the history of this country that covers the Indians, especially the Cherokees, is a sorry one. Even at the time at least one English soldier was moved enough to record in his journal an example of the unnecessary cruelty on the part of the white man. Theda Perdue quotes him in her book *The Cherokee,*

> We proceeded, by Colonel [James] Grant's orders, to burn the Indian cabins. Some of the men seemed to enjoy this cruel work, laughing heartily at the flames, but to me it appeared a shocking sight. Poor creatures, thought I, we surely need not grudge you such miserable habitations. But when we came, according to orders, to cut down the fields of corn, I could scarcely refrain from tears. Who, without grief, could see the stately stalks with broad green leaves and tasseled shocks, the staff of life, sink under our swords with all their precious load.... I saw everywhere around the footsteps of the little Indian children, where they had lately played under the shade of their rustling corn. When we are gone, thought I, they will return, and peeping through the weeds with tearful eyes, will mark the ghastly ruin where they had so often played.

On the other hand, in the case of the region that now includes Polk County, there was some attempt at peaceful coexistence. William Tryon, who governed North Carolina by royal appointment from 1764 to 1771, did his best. His intentions were good. He negotiated a fair-sounding treaty with the Indians and established a border. But in the end it was useless. There were raids and counter attacks, and in the end the Indians were driven out entirely.

Although he was governor of North Carolina for only seven years, Tryon left his mark. The people in what was to become Polk County were so grateful for his help with the Indian problem that they named the highest nearby mountain Tryon Peak.

That was their way of showing gratitude, they thought. But no good deed goes unpunished. Just a few years later, when the movement toward independence was just barely beginning, Governor Tryon put down with severity any activity in that direction. He was so relentless that when the Revolutionary War was in full swing, he was put in command of a corps of Loyalists in New England and promptly burned Danbury, Connecticut, down to the ground—and threw in nearby Fairfield and Norwalk for good measure.

In spite of all that, his former enemies in North Carolina continued to honor him even after the war was over. In 1878 they named the frontier post office Tryon, the name that has persisted to this day.

At least when the authorities had chosen a name for the county in 1855, they had the good sense to name it after someone who had fought on our side, not the enemy's. It is named for the American Revolutionary War hero, Colonel William Polk. The county seat, Columbus, was incorporated in 1857 and named for the county's most tireless civic leader, Dr. Columbus Mills.

As to the town of Saluda, that was not its original name. At first it was called Pace's Gap and was just a crossroads with a few homesteads scattered nearby. A road had been in existence there from the earliest pioneer days as it was the only way—or certainly the best way—through the gap in the mountains for drovers and traders to use. As early as 1800 members of the Pace family began to settle along that road. According to *Polk County, North Carolina History*, the first family named Pace "built an inn with a fenced-in yard so that stock could be penned up for the night while the drovers slept."

The Paces were a prolific family, and today there are so many of them in the area that some Paces don't even know their distant relatives who bear the same name.

In the 1870s when the railroad was being planned, two possible routes were considered: through Howard Gap and through Pace's Gap. Although Pace's Gap was much the steeper of the two, the engineers chose it because "a shifting roadbed caused by underground springs" made the Howard Gap route even more precarious than the other. As a result, Pace's Gap became famous, or infamous if you will, for being the steepest mainline standard gauge grade in the United States.

The number of accidents caused by out-of-control trains is unknown, but there were a lot. Nevertheless, various precautions were taken; the railroad served its purpose and was a success, especially for summer visitors who, even before the railroad was installed, had begun to come by stagecoach from the low country to the cooler mountains. Upon completion of the railroad in 1878 they could now come quickly and easily. And come they did. Pace's Gap prospered.

In 1881 it was chartered as the town of Saluda, named after Saluda mountain, or the Saluda River, which are said to be named for a Cherokee chief whose name meant Corn River. Saluda was the second town to be incorporated in Polk County and it grew. Just as the town was growing, so was a family named Holbert growing.

As early as 1821 we hear of Holberts in the area. The first Holberts to come chose a mountain cove, which became known as Holbert's Cove. A cove, which many people think of as an inlet or bay along a seashore, is also defined in the dictionary as "a small valley between mountains." And that's what Holbert Cove is. Incidentally when the road along this cove was officially named, the apostrophe and the *s* were dropped so that today it is Holbert Cove, which is used in this account for the sake of uniformity.

The Holbert family increased and multiplied so rapidly that no one today can count all the descendants. The Polk County telephone directories alone list no fewer than fifteen families with the name Holbert, none ironically with a Holbert Cove address. But in the 1800s there were any number of Holberts who did live on the road, and by the end of the century many other families had moved in, families with names like Thompson, Pace, and Bradley. John Hiram Johnson was one of these.

TWO

CHAPTER TWO

The Johnson Years

We don't know a great deal about John Johnson's early years. What we do know comes from the scanty and often incomplete official records of the time. He was born on February 27, 1859 in Polk County, exactly where we don't know. His father, Isaac Johnson, was also born in the county, and again we don't know where. We do know, however, that John Johnson was friendly with the most prosperous families in the area because he married into one of them, the Bradley family—twice.

He married young, and he married well. He was only eighteen when he married Winnie Bradley, whose family owned large tracts of land in Polk County on both sides of the Green River, including the land in Holbert Cove where the spectacular (and dangerous) Cove Creek waterfalls are. To this day they are called Bradley Falls. They are incidentally a favorite destination of hikers and are unfortunately also the site of frequent hiking accidents—some fatal.

Winnie Bradley and John Johnson were married on December 2, 1877 and are said to have lived in a cabin about a mile from the Bradley place. Four years after their marriage, on March 29, 1881, their only child was born. She was christened Mary Magdalene Johnson and was called Maggie. When she was only five years old, her mother died (October 29, 1886), possibly of typhoid fever. She was buried in the cemetery at Friendship Baptist Church near Saluda. The grave is still there—unmarked.

Then a curious thing happened. At least it seems strange to us. Less than four months later (February 26, 1887) John Johnson married Sarah Ellen (Sallie) Bradley, age nineteen, who was certainly a relative, and may even have been a sister, of his first wife. They eloped, and local lore has it that when they went to tell Sallie's widowed father, he would not let her in. He just threw her clothes at her. She was his oldest daughter and he was counting on her to be his housekeeper and surrogate mother for the younger children.

What is strange is not so much the haste in which they married, but what the newly married couple did with his child. Little Maggie Johnson did not live with her father and stepmother. She was sent away to relatives to be brought up, not far away, to be sure, but still not with her father. Nevertheless, there was clearly no animosity involved because Johnson and his little daughter were always on excellent terms. Even when she grew up and married, her husband and her father continued the close relationship, living near each other and even sharing several tracts of land they purchased together.

To go back to John Johnson's marriage to Sallie Bradley only four months after he was widowed, the house he built, or more likely was in the process of building before his first wife took sick, was ready for occupancy. The newly married couple moved in immediately. Whether all the outbuildings were ready or whether some of them came later is not known. The outhouse, or privy, which was just a little way beyond the back of

Photo by Stuart Baldwin
Smoke house and chimney

the house, was probably in place from the beginning. The barn, smokehouse, pig pen, and spring house may have come later.

The spring he tapped is worth mentioning. The first thing a homesteader had to do was locate a source of good water, and John Johnson was lucky, probably canny is the better word, in finding the most beautiful spring possible. It still gushes forth water so pure and sweet that when it is tested, which is now done annually, it astonishes the people who test it.

From the beginning, John Johnson farmed the land. Like the other farmers in the area, he was a subsistence farmer, raising all he needed to feed his family and his cattle. In addition, he doubtless had other sources of cash, mainly from an apple orchard near the house and probably also from any surplus of other produce, such as tomatoes and corn.

Photo by Davyd Hood
The smoke house

Thus over the years he was able to acquire more land near his house. Ultimately he owned about 200 acres, although most of it, being steep mountain land, was not useful for farming. I asked an old timer, Etta Thompson Johnson, a neighbor and a relative by marriage of John Johnson, what people like John Johnson did when they needed money—for example, for shoes.

"Oh," she said, "they made their own shoes way back then." And, indeed, we later found iron lasts and forms for tiny children's shoes up through adult sizes that someone had

Iron shoe lasts

used on the premises. These lasts are now on exhibit in the old house.

"But surely," I persisted, "they needed money sometimes."

Photo by Don Wilson

Clothes press made by John Johnson for his bride, Sallie

Photo by Jack Hahn

Chairs made by John Johnson. Notice the hand-carved finials.

"Then," said Etta, "they would find a long, straight tree and cut it down, and sell it for railroad ties." So we see that some ready cash was available, but not much.

After a dozen years or so, around 1900, it appears that Johnson partially gave up farming his mountain land and took other jobs in the area. He and Sallie were still childless. His daughter by his first marriage, Maggie, was by the standards of the time a grown woman. She had been married in 1898 at age seventeen to Jack Newman and was starting a family of her own. At this point John Johnson decided to work elsewhere, and almost certainly he worked at Ricks (frequently misspelled Rix) Haven.

Ricks Haven

Ricks Haven was, and what's left of it still is, on a shoulder of Tryon Peak, almost directly opposite John Johnson's house, only about a mile as the crow flies. To walk there, or to go by mule, would have taken about an hour as the mountain paths in that area are steep and circuitous. To go there by road would have taken much longer as it is many miles in length, twisting and turning its way up to Mrs. Ricks' house.

It is possible Johnson could have walked there daily, at best a tough exercise. Or he could have occupied one of at least two houses Mrs. Ricks built on the premises, presumably for workers. In any case he was getting paid for work he was doing for someone, and if it was for Mrs. Ricks, he was not alone. "Almost everyone around here worked for Mrs. Ricks at one time or another," I was told by Simp Thompson, a neighbor of the Johnsons. "My brother Buck worked there for a while—walked up there and back. She paid him one dollar for a day's work." She needed a lot of help because she was running the biggest agricultural and animal husbandry operation that ever took place in this area, before or since.

There is a certain amount of mystery surrounding the Ricks Haven story. No one seems certain about when Mrs. Ricks arrived or how she acquired the seed money to start her enterprise. County records show that she began buying up land in 1908. In fifteen different transactions over the next ten years, she acquired 2166½ acres plus three lots of less than one acre each.

No one knows where Mrs. Ricks came from. Some say, "Yazoo City, Mississippi;" some simply say, "She came from off." Herbert E. Pace, writing in 1983 in the *Polk County, North Carolina History* says this:

> Years ago Fanny J. Rix [sic] of Yazoo City, Miss., came to Saluda, bought some land on Tryon Mountain, and first lived in a tent, then built a small

house. J.S. Arledge told me his father, the Rev. J.S. Arledge, built more to the small house of chestnut logs. Mr. Arledge said she bought land from Jimmie Price, Ed Bradley, Dick Petty, Joe and Will Raines, a speculation company and others. Mrs. Rix owned about 1,700 acres—had about 1,600 under fence.

She did a lot of farming, had all kinds of horse-drawn machinery; had a team of mules and team of horses. She had about 100 head of Angora goats, 100 head of purebred sheep, a herd of Red Devon cattle, some purebred Tamworth hogs, a flock of chickens, and a horse which she drove to the buggy.

Mrs. Rix worked a lot of people. She raised a lot of corn, and had a corn shredder. She raised rye, oats, vetch, barley, velvet beans and most everything she needed to eat and for feed. Mrs. Rix had her stock shipped by train to Saluda and drove them over the road to the mountain. Mr. Arledge worked for Mrs. Rix. He said she brought a colored man with her from Mississippi to help around the house (also a German girl).

Mrs. Rix got water from a deep well with a wind mill. She later built a big house farther up the mountain and called this "Rix Haven." She did her own road surveying.

The colored man that worked for Mrs. Rix went back to Mississippi and got killed. Mrs. Rix and the German girl died on the mountain about 1918.

Some say that Mrs. Ricks got the "milk sick" from tainted milk. Charles O. Hearon, Jr. in his book, *I Remember Saluda*, says that the milk sick "was something caused by drinking milk from a cow that had been grazing on the north side of the mountain." Whether Mrs. Ricks and her companion died at Ricks Haven or went back to Mississippi is unclear. What is certain is that Ricks Haven was abandoned. Old timers say that for a while there was a caretaker, but he soon left and the place fell into disrepair. The house was empty for a number of years until mysteriously (because no one was supposed to be on the premises) it burnt to the ground.

It was later acquired by Carl Story, county commissioner for Polk County. He passed it on to his son, Jack Story, who still owns it. Part of the land is being developed as a subdivision, while the ruin of the old house is, at this writing, just that—a ruin.

But in its heyday, it hummed with activity and success, and as we have said John Johnson was almost certainly one of her employees. In 1910 the national census was taken, and we learn from it that he had then three dependents, a wife and two children, and that he is listed as a farmer and a manager. In addition to his wife, Sallie, the record includes their two daughters, Naomi, born on September 19, 1906, (incorrectly spelled *Naomia*) and Fannie, only three months old, born on January 8, 1910 (incorrectly spelled *Fanny*).

It was just about this time that John Johnson and his son-in-law, Jackson (Jack) Newman, were involved in at least three land acquisitions, indicating that Johnson had some sort of paying job. In 1900 they bought 175 acres for $460, and three years later, another 190 acres on Little Cove Creek. Altogether they bought 365 acres, all contiguous with the land on which Johnson's house stood. Family tradition has it that Jack Newman and his wife, Maggie Johnson Newman (John Johnson's daughter by his first wife) built a house, or cabin, on

John H. Johnson and his family: Fannie, Sallie, and Naomi

her father's property right after their marriage in 1898. There are the remains of an old chimney still visible in a beautiful wooded area alongside a spring that flows into Little Cove Creek, but no one seems certain if this was the Newman house or if it was elsewhere. Everyone agrees, however, that Maggie and Jack Newman lived near her father and stepmother for a few years and later moved to a permanent home about a mile from the Johnson house. We'll meet them later and continue their story because it ties in with the old home place.

In the meantime John Johnson was ready to give up his house and his farm on Holbert Cove Road and his job with Mrs. Ricks, and move on. He had lived in the old house for two decades, he had a wife and two daughters, and had earned enough money to buy forty-six acres of land in Henderson County for $2,000, where he moved in 1910. Four years later he took a job as superintendent of the Henderson County Home for indigents and sold all his property in Polk County including the house on Holbert Cove Road. We have only one picture of John Johnson and it was taken about this time. He is with his wife and two little girls, a handsome family. The parents look strong, the kind of people who could be counted on, trustworthy and honest in their plain clothes. The little girls are wearing gingham dresses, undoubtedly made by their mother.

His good fortune did not last long, however. He died on May 11, 1917 at the age of fifty-eight. His widow was forty-nine, and his daughters, Naomi and Fannie, were only ten and seven. His body was taken back to Polk County to the cemetery at Friendship Baptist Church, where he is buried next to his first wife's unmarked grave. His headstone is a pretty one with a rounded top, to the right of an identical headstone where his wife Sallie would be buried twenty-three years later. She and the two little girls stayed on in Henderson County until the end.

It is at this point that we leave the John Hiram Johnson family temporarily because they have no further contact with the old home place for more than three-quarters of a century—seventy-nine years to be exact.

What happened then, seventy-nine years later, will be related in its own good time. In the meanwhile, we'll hear about the second family to live in the old home place, the Sherfys.

Photo by Hazel Jaeger

Sallie and John Johnson's graves

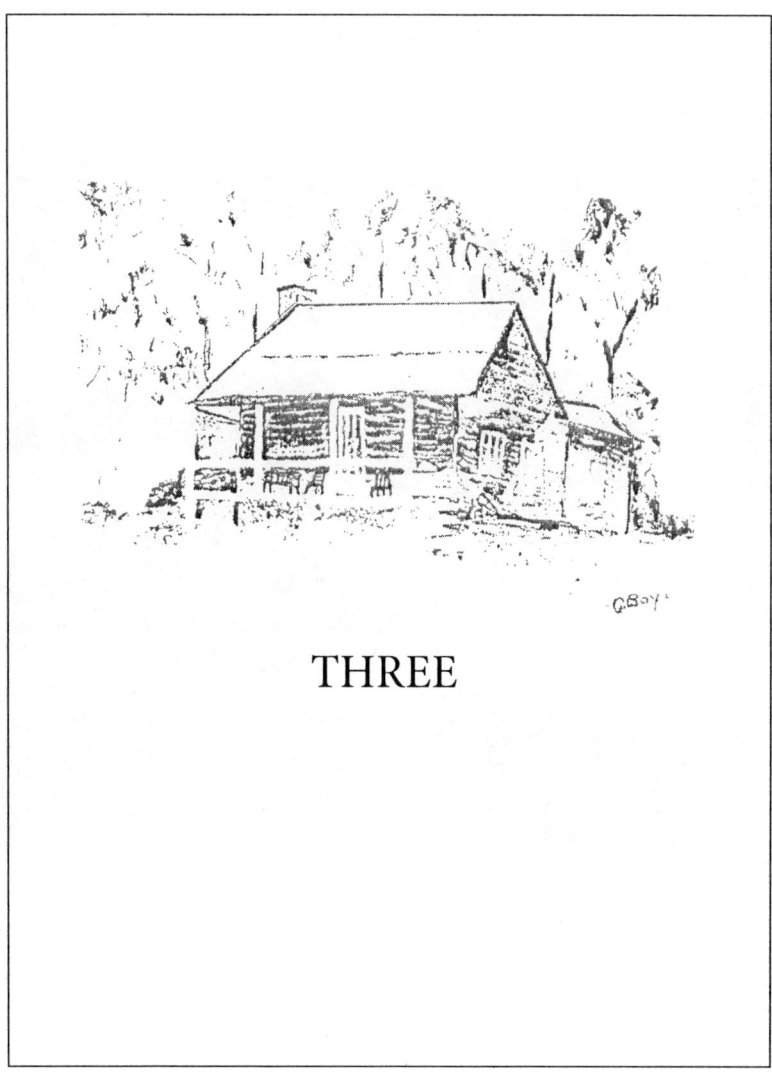

THREE

*The Sherfy family. Front row: Maggie, Virginia, Rev. Joel Sherfy
Back row: Mary, Leona*

CHAPTER THREE

The Sherfy Years

When John Johnson and his family moved to Henderson County in 1910, Joel Sherfy moved in. Always called Rev. Sherfy, he had a wife and three teen-age daughters. He was sixty-nine years old when he made the move and what prompted him to do so, at that age, is unknown. We have a picture of him and his family taken about the time they moved, or a little later, but it was clearly not taken at the old house. In those days people went to a photographer's studio, dressed in their finest clothes, for a memorable photo. In this one they are a handsome group, especially the father with his impressive white beard, proud of his good-looking wife and three lovely daughters.

He doesn't look like the kind of man who sweated over a plow, but he is said to have been a farmer before and after he came to Holbert Cove Road. In addition, he pursued his vocation, or avocation, as a minister in the Church of the Brethren. His background before coming to Polk County is somewhat hazy. We have no record of where he and his wife were born, but we do know that they had tried living in Tennessee, and then Florida, before moving to North Carolina. His wife's maiden name was Margaret (Maggie) Green and his daughters were Leona, Mary May, and Virginia.

Incidentally, in the old days, names ending in *a* were pronounced as if they ended in *y*. Thus Leona was pronounced Leony; Saluda was pronounced Saludy, and Etta, Etty. Today you rarely hear these quaint pronunciations of the past, not to mention the archaic word usage of the back country that used to be so prevalent. Radio and the movies started the homogenization of language, and television is finally erasing all regional accents entirely, especially in rural America. More's the pity.

The Sherfy family settled in—all five of them, and it must have been a tight squeeze because there were only two small bedrooms (7'4" x 8'1") in the house and no closets whatsoever. We have to guess that the three girls slept together in one of the bedrooms, and their parents in the other. The house at that time consisted only of the main room with the fireplace (which, incidentally, smoked badly) and the two bedrooms with the cooking done in a side room, known as the cooking room. What was later to become the kitchen was only an open area, or at most an open porch. It was not enclosed and fitted with a stove until after the Sherfy family left , about seven years later.

Joel Sherfy was a tenant for the first four years he lived in the old house. By 1914 John Johnson was well-established in Hendersonville and ready to sell his house and property in Polk County. Sherfy bought it for $1,500, the house and 216.50 acres. He was seventy-three years old and apparently beginning to worry about the future of his family because he made plans for them. He had the land surveyed and divided into four lots, presumably for his wife and three daughters. As it turned out, he was to be around for another sixteen years, living to the then almost unheard of advanced age of eighty-nine.

But long before that, maybe even before the land was surveyed and divided into lots, his daughters had begun to move away. Leona, the oldest, married Clifford Gilbert and moved to Florida; Virginia married Marvin Edwards and moved to Tryon; and only Mary, the middle daughter, remained. She was not married until a year or so later, and in the meanwhile she was the teacher in a nearby elementary school.

The Rev. Sherfy didn't preach at the nearby Mt. Lebanon church on Holbert Cove Road—or indeed at any Baptist church, and this leads to an interesting tale. He preached at a church some distance away. It so happened—or more likely it was very carefully planned—that one Sunday when he was away preaching, his only child still living at home, Mary May Sherfy, had plans of her own. The plans included a handsome young man named Curtis Garrett, her suitor from Mill Spring.

Taking advantage of her father's absence, they were married at the Friendship Baptist Church at the west end of Holbert Cove Road near Saluda. It was June 20, 1915. Her mother and some other witnesses were present, but her father, the Rev. Sherfy, was deliberately omitted. Although the plans had been kept secret from him, we know that they had not been kept secret from the neighborhood at large because someone came up to him after his sermon that Sunday and said, "When you get home, you're going to find out you have a new son-in-law." Mary Sherfy Garrett was eighteen; Curtis Garrett was nineteen.

Why the secrecy, or rather why was the wedding kept secret from the father and not the mother? No one seems to know except that often we hear of a father who took exception to one of his daughter's suitors and who vigorously (sometimes with a gun) discouraged the would-be bridegroom. In any case the marriage of Mary Sherfy to Curtis Garrett took place, and the Rev. Sherfy could not have been too upset because thereafter the young couple lived on his land, probably in a cabin, and soon after that his house and land were deeded to the young Garretts.

Joel and Maggie Sherfy moved to a house nearer Saluda, where they lived until his death on January 18, 1930. For the next twenty-three years Mrs. Sherfy divided her time among her daughters until her death at age ninety-three (July 22, 1953). Both she and her husband are buried in the graveyard of the Friendship Baptist Church.

Long before that their house became known as the Garrett house. The Garretts, or their children, owned it for over sixty years. Longer than anyone else, and a new chapter begins.

*Margaret (Maggie) Green Sherfy lived
to be ninety-three.*

FOUR

Mary Sherfy Garrett

CHAPTER FOUR

The Garrett Years

Curtis and Mary Garrett settled in the old home place about the time their first child, Raymond, was born in 1917. Curtis Garrett took over the farming operation, raising the usual crops, corn and vegetables for his family, and feed for his livestock, which included a cow, a mule, pigs, chickens, and children. They ultimately had three, two boys and a girl.

They had plenty to eat but not much else. Occasionally Garrett took the mule and wagon, which was filled with produce, and sold it in nearby communities, especially in Saluda. Saluda became known as a popular, though always low-key, summer resort. Every summer the population swelled with the many families who came up from the low country for the cooler mountain air. But except for money earned from produce and a few dollars Mary Garrett earned making patchwork quilts, there was little ready cash. But enough to get by. The children all had shoes, all attended school regularly, and all had friends nearby for companionship.

Although the family lived only five miles from the town of Saluda, neither they nor most of the people who lived in Holbert Cove were directly involved in many—or any—of the activities that drew the summer visitors. In addition to the climate and the pleasures and parties that the outsiders enjoyed, there was another attraction that drew visitors to Saluda. It is worth mentioning because it was a collection of establishments that became nationally, even internationally, recognized in the field of pediatric medicine. From a small beginning pediatrics in Saluda grew and flourished for more than thirty years. There were three affiliated institutions: the Infants' and Children's Sanitarium, founded by Dr. D. Lesesne Smith in 1914; a baby hospital for poor children, founded the same year by a group of civic leaders from Spartanburg; and a few years later, the Southern Pediatric Seminar, a post-graduate course for pediatricians.

Dr. Smith, who had been practicing medicine in Spartanburg, South Carolina, for a number of years observed that babies who were sickening and dying in the summer heat of the low country and elsewhere could be saved if they were moved. He postulated that what was needed was proper care in a cooler, more salubrious climate. The ideal place from his point of view was his and his wife's summer home, which was on a hilltop just above Main Street in Saluda. So with only eighteen patients at first, he began his sanitarium on that hilltop, which came to be known as Smith Hill.

At the same time that Dr. Smith was planning his sanitarium, Charles Hearon, editor of the *Spartanburg Herald*, began promoting the establishment of a free hospital for poor children. A philanthropist answered the call, a hospital committee was formed, and the Spartanburg Baby Hospital was on its way. The place chosen for the free hospital was a house just opposite the stores on Main Street, only a short distance from Dr. Smith's place. Dr. Smith gave his services without charge to the hospital, and the Spartanburg people paid all the other costs. The patients paid nothing.

By 1921 when there were enough cases to serve as clinical material, the Southern Pediatric Seminar was instituted. As word spread doctors came from all parts of the South and elsewhere to learn about the diagnosis and treatment of children's diseases. It is estimated that between three and four thousand doctors attended the sessions, some of them returning many times, and the number of little sick children who got well from all these efforts cannot even be estimated.

In its final form more than a dozen frame buildings housed the personnel, the visiting doctors, the sick children, and members of Dr. Smith's family. All of them including his four children helped out, and when they grew up and married, their husbands and wives joined in. They provided a valuable service not only for the patients, but for medicine in general.

After WW II ended in 1945, air conditioning became almost universal and hence the importance of moving sickly children to a cooler climate was lessened. Dr. Smith died in 1947, and a few years later the hospital and the sanitarium closed their doors. By the end of the 1950s when pediatric medicine had come of age and the need for a training course for doctors had diminished, the seminar closed its doors too. Dr. Smith's children, and ultimately his grandchildren, inherited the buildings and today are lovingly restoring them.

During all these years, Charles Hearon, the man who had promoted the funding for the free hospital for sick babies, continued to come to Saluda every summer with his family. Their place was on Holbert Cove Road, and they were the only family on that road who did not live there year round. But that was no drawback—they had been coming there since 1913 and they fit right in. There were four children, two boys and two girls, and one of them, Charles O. Hearon, Jr. (C. Boy) loved Saluda with such intensity that he wrote a book about it and lives there still, at least during the summer.

His book, which includes a dozen or so of his pencil sketches, is called *I Remember Saluda, A Storytelling*. It is a series of vignettes of the people and places he came to know and love, told with such ease and warmth that you can't help catching the flavor of that simple, wholesome place and those gentle times between the two world wars. His sketch of the old home place, which appears throughout this book, is an example of his art work.

It was summer people like the Hearons and the activities on Smith Hill that helped Saluda survive the great depression. The population rose from a few hundred year-round residents to several thousand visitors every summer, and with them came a degree of prosperity, which extended, as we have seen, to the people who lived in Holbert Cove.

There was one other source of income that deserves to be mentioned, a source of income that to this day no one will discuss openly. This was a thriving moonshine industry. No one, even then, could tell how many distilleries, or stills, were hidden away in the hills, but there were plenty of them. We have pictures of one such still that was almost certainly near the old home place. The owners were readily identified, and we have been assured that this was not the only one nearby. "The woods were full of them."

Prohibition lasted from 1920 to 1933. Although stills were most prevalent during these years, whiskey making started long before that and continued well after. As late as the 1980s someone gave us a gift of white lightning in a mayonnaise jar and it

A rare picture taken during Prohibition of a still near the old home place

Another picture of the still near the old home place. The identity of the men, though known, may not yet be revealed for fear of revenuers. (One of the men pictured here later became a preacher)

was potent, like firecrackers going off in your throat and rockets in your head. If you're dumb enough to ask, people will tell you it was used for medicinal purposes. In his book *Sights and Sounds in Saluda*, Herman Nodine quotes an old timer who said his mama lived to be ninety years old and never needed glasses. "She would just always drink straight from the jug."

To get back to the Garrett family at the old home place, Curtis Garrett was probably not involved in that thriving cottage industry. We know that for a little extra cash he would load up his wagon with his surplus produce—corn, tomatoes, and potatoes—hitch up his mule, and head for Saluda. But he did not profit hugely. In fact, at one point he moved his family out of the old house to one closer to Saluda and was employed

The barn   *Photo by Don Wilson*

Photo by Stuart Baldwin
View of the barn from the porch. The original barn built by John Johnson was replaced by this one.

Photo by Jack Hahn
The shed

at one of the nearby vineyards, grapes being a big item in the economy of Polk County at that time. Growers often hired foremen or managers year round, and extra workers at harvest time. For several years Garrett was hired as one of the year-round managers.

His first two children, Raymond and Hubert were born in the old house, but when his third child and only daughter, Ruby, was born in 1924, the family was living in the house near Saluda, which is no longer standing. The Garretts lived in that house until Ruby was seven years old when the family moved back to the old home place. They moved because the grape-growing industry in Saluda had ceased.

Why this once profitable crop failed is something of a mystery. Some say a blight caused the vines to wither and die. Some say there was no market for the grapes. Whatever the reason,

Photo by Don Wilson
Washstand and pitcher from the Garrett years

Mary Garrett's pitcher and bowl

the Garrett family once more installed themselves in the old home place and the children attended the Mt. Lebanon School, walking the two miles there and back in all weather. Raymond and Hubert went as far as the sixth grade and Ruby finished seventh grade.

Life at the old home place cannot be described adequately without mention of some of the neighbors. The nearest were the Buck Thompsons, who lived a half-mile up the road toward Saluda. They had twelve children, two by Thompsons's first wife, Mattie Garrett, who died, and ten by his second wife,

Handmade steps to the attic

Molly Garrett, Mattie's sister. Curtis Garrett was their brother. Buck and Mattie's children were Essie and Mamie. Buck and Molly's children were:

NAME	BIRTH AND DEATH DATES
Etta	1899 - 1991
Hoyt	Jan. 1900 - 1986
Ragan	Dec. 1900 - 1970
Buck	1902 - 1993
Gay	1905 - 1993
Horace	1907 - 1993
Robert	1911 - 1934
Simp	1913 -
Annie	1915 -
Fred	1918 -

Etta Thompson Johnson in her eighties

Annie Thompson

Their house was built in the 1890s and was still in use up to 1984. Horace Thompson was living there alone. He liked to keep his house good and warm, a luxury none of these houses had afforded in the old days. But with the availability of effective new wood stoves, you could keep even an old drafty house comfortably hot, so Horace had installed one of the most efficient of this new breed of stoves, a Fisher. Fisher Stoves came in three sizes, called affectionately Papa Bear, Mama Bear, and Baby Bear. Horace had a Papa Bear.

The old Thompson house with its plain stone chimney, framed with wood and mortared with mud, didn't have a chance of withstanding the intense heat his stove generated. Sooner or later the old dry wood was going to ignite and the house catch fire like a tinder box. There must have been dozens of houses nearby that suffered the same fate, and as a result almost no old houses remain if they have not been adjusted to accommodate such stoves, primarily by metal liners (preferably stainless steel) in the chimney.

The Thompson house had no liner whatsoever, and on the night of November 25, 1984 the house burned to the ground. Luckily Horace got out safely, but not a vestige of the house remained. It has since been replaced by what is called in the trade a manufactured home but is generally known as a double wide, meaning a trailer twice as wide as usual. It is stained a natural wood color and is more attractive than most, especially since Annie Thompson, who now lives there, keeps it in apple pie order. Horace Thompson lived there until his death in 1993.

Among the many children who lived on Holbert Cove Road was Hazel Johnson, Ruby Garrett's special friend and cousin. She was the daughter of Etta Thompson and Gaither Johnson, who lived in the red house on top of the hill about a mile toward Saluda. That house, built in 1893, is still standing but was modernized long ago.

Hazel Johnson, now Jaeger, still owns the house, though she lives elsewhere. She was an only child and says, "I was four years younger than Ruby, and I was in and out of their house every day. I used to stay for dinner, which we all ate together at the table in their kitchen. I loved being with the Garrett family."

The children had a wealth of ways to entertain themselves. The boys rambled in the woods at will, hunting and fishing when they were old enough. "We ate possum and squirrel," they say. As younger children they played the same games children played everywhere, hide and seek, running games, ball

Ruby Garrett, age 13

games, marbles, and horse shoes. The girls played with dolls. There was never any lack of companionship.

In addition to the Thompsons and Johnsons on Holbert Cove Road, there was another family that was to play a large part in the story of the old home place. This was the Newman family who lived about a mile down the road going toward Mill Spring. You'll recall that John Johnson's first child, Maggie, whose mother had died when she was a toddler, married Jackson (Jack) Newman in 1898, and at first lived on her father's property in a cabin. They stayed in that cabin only a few years before moving to the new house Jack Newman was building a mile away.

This couple, Jack and Maggie Johnson Newman, had thirteen children. The first three, Belcher, Barnard, and a baby boy, all of whom died in infancy, were probably born in the cabin mentioned earlier on the John Johnson property. All the others were born in the house Jack Newman built on his own land. They were:

NAME	BIRTH AND DEATH DATES
Orpha	1903 - 1991
Shadrach (Shake)	1905 - 1970
Geneva	1908 -
Winston Salem (Jim)	1910 - 1973
Thadford (Thad)	1912 - 1990
Blease	1914 - 1992
Loftis (Deek)	1916 - 1994
Freda	1919 *(died in childhood)*
George	1921 *(died in childhood)*
Annie Lee	1922 - 1992

Curtis and Mary Garrett, about 1941 or 1942

With eight Newman children and ten Thompson children, not to mention the other families who lived in the Cove, the Garrett children were never deprived of companionship. It was a happy rural existence.

All that changed on December 7, 1941. The world would never be the same again, and Holbert Cove Road was no exception. The United States entered WW II, and all the eligible men went into various branches of the military. The Thompson family alone had six boys in uniform. Both of the Garrett boys joined and were sent overseas, Raymond to North Africa, and then Italy, Hubert to India. Deek Newman, the only eligible one in that family, was in Patton's Third Army in Europe.

Raymond Garrett, World War II photo

Hubert Garrett, World War II photo

    In the meanwhile Ruby Garrett got a job in the hosiery mill in Saluda where she worked until after the war was over. And miraculously all the young men from the Cove who had served overseas returned safely. Deek Newman was the only one who suffered any long-term disability. Even though he had not been wounded on the battlefield, he had contracted pneumonia while in training for the Army in Michigan and was hospitalized. Unfortunately he was discharged from the infirmary without proper restrictions before he had completely recovered. As a result he was forced to resume rigorous training immediately, which included an overnight hike in cold, damp weather, which in turn resulted in a relapse, and ultimately the loss of one lung. He suffered from that inexcusable accident for the rest of his life, and the Army had to pay for his disability, a waste all around.

Finally the war was over and everyone returned to the Cove, but not for long. It was inevitable that the old families, like families everywhere, began to scatter. Marriages and jobs elsewhere took many of them away from the Cove. Raymond married Katherine McKaig and moved to Tryon. Hubert stayed in the Army for eighteen years. Most of the Thompson young people left, as did the Newmans, Deek Newman being the only member of that family who continued to live in his family's home place. Ruby Garrett still lived with her family a mile away. And therein hangs a tale.

Deek and Ruby

There was never a time that Ruby Garrett did not know the entire Newman family. They were neighbors and schoolmates, all at one time or another attending the Mount Lebanon School. Deek, being six years older than Ruby, was of course too old to be a playmate when she was a child, and by the time she grew up enough to be noticed, he was in the Army and overseas. But when he returned, it was a different matter. She was twenty-one and very attractive.

Bit by bit they became friends and then more than friends, and then finally engaged. But Ruby hesitated to take the final step; she was reluctant even to tell her parents that she was interested in marriage. This went on for years until finally Deek decided he would wait no longer. He gave an ultimatum. The marriage was to take place on Friday, August 5, 1960 or there would be no marriage. Ruby agreed and plans were made, but no one was let in on the secret.

Deek and Ruby Newman, 1989 photo

Ruby went to Spartanburg and bought a new dress, white shoes, and a white purse with money she had earned at the hosiery mill. The dress was a pretty soft blue with a bow at the collar—Deek had asked her to wear a blue dress. Then she had her hair shampooed. While this was going on Deek polished his shoes and went to the barbershop in Saluda. Someone saw him there and wondered out loud why he was sprucing himself up, and even asked some pointed questions, but Deek, never a man of many words, evaded the issue. Ruby, meanwhile, announced she was spending the night with a friend, a perfectly honest statement.

Deek had it planned to the last detail. They would drive the thirty-five or forty miles to Spartanburg and get married in the courthouse there, then spend the night in nearby Marion, North Carolina. They would face Ruby's family after the deed was done.

"But why did you have to be married so secretly?" I asked Deek years later. "Why did you elope?"

"We had to," he replied.

"But why?" I persisted. "Did you think Ruby's father would try to prevent you from getting married?"

"I didn't think; I knew," Deek replied. "If we had told him ahead of time, he would have got his gun and sent me out of there."

Ruby agrees. So at about three o'clock in the afternoon, they slipped out and went to Spartanburg. The next day they returned to Deek's house.

The house, which is at 81 Holbert Cove Road, was built a few years before to replace the fifty-year-old house that had been there since shortly after his parents' marriage. The original house had fallen into bad repair, so a few years before his mother's death, Deek, with some help from his brothers, had built a new and better house next to the old one. He had then demolished the old house. His father had died some years before, and upon his mother's death in 1950 Deek acquired the house and the land. He was free to marry if he chose. And he chose.

It was the perfect setting for a new bride, especially for Ruby as she would be only a mile from her parents. There was, nevertheless, a certain amount of awkwardness, to say the least, when she faced her parents. But even they could not deny that her situation was ideal.

They had to admit furthermore, that Deek was the ideal son-in-law. It took no time at all before they were reconciled and ultimately delighted. They saw their daughter daily and Deek helped them in hundreds of ways. This amiable relationship remained until their deaths.

To go back to the 1950s, though, it is necessary to mention a momentous event that occurred in the Cove—an event that affected every single household on Holbert Cove Road—except one. On March 8, 1954, electricity finally was made available in that remote area. The people were joyous. No more kerosene lanterns, no more cold houses heated only by logs, no more cooking on a wood stove.

The only exception was the family at the old home place. Curtis Garrett refused to put in, and put up with, any such modern devices. No matter if all his neighbors were elated, he would march to a different drummer. And a good thing it was too.

When you reflect that for almost half a century the rest of America had enjoyed the amenities that electricity made possible, you can realize how eager the people on Holbert Cove Road were to live like everyone else. Houses were modernized immediately. Electric lights blazed. Electric stoves were installed. Telephones were anticipated (although they didn't get there until August 26, 1966). And even central heat became a possibility.

Not so for the Garretts. And thank goodness, for their house is the only year-round house in all of western North Carolina, as far as we can determine, that remains exactly as it was in 1887, up to the present day (1997 at this writing). All other such houses were electrified or have telephones and, in effect, ruined from a historical point of view. There is no way, as we near the 21st century, that we can really experience life in the nineteenth and yet at the same time enjoy indoor plumbing and instant heat and light.

Every family who had lived there—the Johnsons, the Sherfys, and the Garretts—all had done their part (whether deliberately or inadvertently) in saving this little bit of history. But all that was almost obliterated by ignorance on the part of the next owners. The house was a hair's breadth away from being demolished.

Photo by Jack Hahn

FIVE

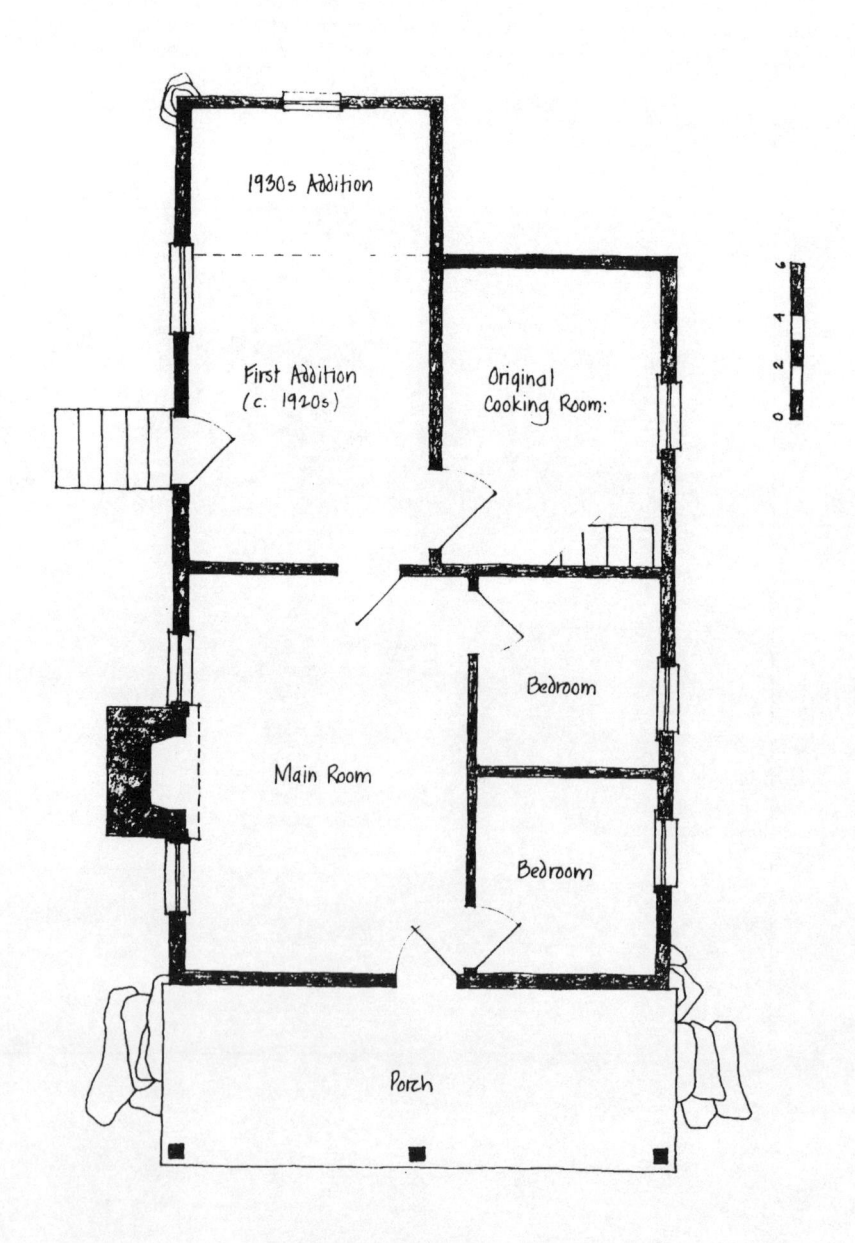

Plan by Anne McCutcheon Lewis, FAIA.

CHAPTER FIVE

The McCutcheon Years

I don't mind admitting that we were somewhat smart alecky when we arrived. We are smart alecks no longer. Now we are respectful enough to appreciate what has gone before. We are humble and not ashamed of being so.

My husband, John (Jack) McCutcheon, who had been the editorial page editor of the *Chicago Tribune* for a dozen years, and I, who had been a nationally syndicated columnist, were in the process of retiring to a less hectic way of life and a more benign climate than that of Lake Forest, Illinois.

We had looked in Arkansas; in Gatlinburg, Tennessee; and in North Carolina—Highlands and Tryon. Arkansas was unappealing—cold in the winter and hot and dry in the summer. Gatlinburg was worse. It is one of the great disasters of our time. It must have been beautiful before modern man ruined it with endless tourist attractions—ugly signs, ugly buildings, congestion, and all the rest. The whole town is like the entrance way to almost every American city. Fast food establishments, motels, gas stations, and signs, signs, signs, all trying to outshout the next one. I don't know when people will ever learn.

We liked North Carolina, but Highlands was too cold and Tryon too sophisticated. We wanted mountains to climb and streams to ford. So after looking around, we were reluctantly heading back to Illinois when we happened to pass through Saluda. Here was a plain little country town, unpretentious, not fixed up, and we liked that. As Herman Nodine says in his book *Sights and Sounds in Saluda*, "You are not likely to get lost while window shopping in the downtown business district." Something about the place invites you to loiter. We stopped at old Mr. John Thompson's junk shop (now Nostalgia Courtyard) to look around.

It was he who told us about a lot of open land on Holbert Cove Road, mentioning that he just happened to be a real estate agent on the side. So off we went with him late that beautiful November afternoon, November 20, 1978, to be exact.

He showed us a sixty-acre piece owned at that time by Bobby Joe Stott. We wondered about the two-rut road that went through the land and up the mountain beyond, but Mr. Thompson said he did not know anything about it, which aroused our curiosity.

We liked the land we had seen, but we did not like the possibility of another owner, or several owners for that matter, having access through it, so we went back up north somewhat disappointed. Yet somehow we could not forget Holbert Cove Road. We did some research via county records and found that the land up the mountain was owned by the Garrett family and that the road leading there was theirs to use by common law right. We tried to forget that we had ever seen it.

But by February the following year (1979), we still hadn't forgotten. We decided to go back and explore on our own. We flew to Asheville, rented a car and drove up the lonely two-rut road as far as we could until it became impassable for a car. We

Hubert Garrett on our first visit, 1979

got out and walked. We could hear dogs barking and a man's voice telling them to shut up. That was a good sign.

Up we went, and there suddenly at the top of the hill was the house, the shed, the barn—all in a tumble down condition—and Hubert Garrett—bib overalls, cheerful, friendly. Bless his heart. He showed us all around his place. It was beautiful except for years of neglect and decades of detritus. No matter, we both knew that this was the place for us—someday perhaps.

"If ever we get this place," I said to Jack in an undertone, "the first thing we'd do would be to get rid of this house. We wouldn't need a bulldozer, either. Just a match."

Hubert didn't hear me—and a good thing because he said just then, "My sister's husband, Deek Newman—his grandpa built this house in 1887." Our ears perked up. Jack was (and still is) a trustee of the Chicago Historical Society and I was on the board of directors of the Lake Forest-Lake Bluff Historical Society. Suddenly I could see the house as history, not as a pile of ashes.

Then he added the words that sent us reeling. "It's for sale," he said. "The house and 148 acres."

"Ask him," I whispered to Jack, "where we pay our money." Jack did, but considerably more subtly. Hubert told us that his sister, who lived about a mile down the road, was handling the sale. We thanked him and went, without any delay, to Ruby's house. She heard us drive up.

The door was opened just a crack as we walked up the porch steps. She greeted us, but skeptically. Yes, the land was for sale, but Mr. Newman's nephew had an option on it until March 12, 1979. She closed the door.

Exactly two weeks later we telephoned the Newmans from Lake Forest. Deek answered the phone. "The land is your'n if you want it." We did. But by the time we checked out the right of way and had a lawyer check the deed, and by the time we got our money together, it was not until June 22, 1979, that we actually owned the property. We have never regretted the time, the trouble, and the money it ultimately cost us.

If we had known how many complications lay ahead, we perhaps would not have been so jubilant. Suffice it to say that when each problem arose, we somehow managed to gird our loins and face it.

The problems involved the purchase of a great deal more land contiguous to our property than we ever dreamed of owning but were compelled to buy. If we had not, we would have had to allow a road to be constructed right alongside the old house in order to allow the owners of the land beyond it to reach their property. There is an almost universal law that forbids one land owner from locking out another owner from his property. In other words, you must allow the right to access even if the only way to reach the other person's property is through your front yard, which in this case it would have been. And which, in this case, would have utterly ruined the historic setting of the old home place. Happily, it is now protected, as far as we were able against any future degradation.

In addition to having to buy the land above the old house, we were also faced with the possibility of a large development or trailer park before we reached our property. Actually there was already one unsightly trailer along with its collection of junk and rusting cars that we had to pass on the driveway to our place, and a year or so later another trailer was added. With eleven more acres to go, the owners could have done us in. But luckily about ten years later, they wanted to leave, and we were able to buy their land and get rid of the trailers.

In the meanwhile we were struggling with saving the old house from immediate ruin. The roof leaked, much of the floor was rotted through, and the place was infested with vermin. Besides that, there was almost a century of trash to clear as there had never been any means of disposing of waste other than to throw it down the nearest gully or behind the thickest bush.

We took seven truckloads of trash to the dump and thought we had the place clear, but even now, almost twenty years later, every heavy rain storm washes away a little topsoil and reveals bits of broken glass, an old shoe, pieces of a rusty coffee pot and similar objects. Some of the items are interesting—even somewhat valuable, like the cobalt blue glass bottles we find occasionally.

Photo by Jack Hahn

Wood burning cook stove

But long before we had the place in good shape, we tried sleeping and eating there. Our first night was April 4, 1980—very uncomfortable. We had no cook stove, no adequate light, no heat. One more night and we were out of there and asleep in a nearby motel.

Actually it was not until a year or so later that our visits became longer and our way of life less primitive. We ordered a good wood burning cook stove from the Sears Roebuck catalog, bought kerosene lanterns, and installed an excellent Vermont Castings wood stove that provides adequate heat for the whole house. Above all, we discovered a man who agreed to build us a shower house, a remarkable little log building with all the amenities and yet acceptable to the most exacting environmentalist.

Photo by Don Wilson
The Vermont Castings stove

It is equipped with a system for abundant hot water for the shower and wash basin; it has a composting toilet that is completely sanitary and odor-free; and yet it uses no power whatsoever, save what Mother Nature supplies. The water for the shower flows from the spring by gravity and is heated by scraps of wood fed into a small tank. The toilet is run by friendly bacteria with the help of a sprinkling of peat moss; and a solar panel provides some heat. A small kerosene heater provides the rest, and kerosene lamps attached to the wall provide light.

The brilliant young man who designed and executed all this is a teacher in Hendersonville named Richard Colgan. He designed and built the building of concrete blocks, faced with rustic logs on the exterior, and placed it near enough to the house to be useful, yet out of sight entirely so that it does not detract from the historical authenticity of the old house. It is a few steps down the side of the hill beyond the back door.

Another concession we made to twentieth century technology was to have the old mud and stone chimney lined with a strong stainless steel liner its entire length and extending a little above the chimney top. Anyone interested in saving an old house and yet wanting to keep warm by the latest model wood burning stove ought to consider lining the chimney. The number one reason that few old houses like ours are still standing is that they go up in flames when a good iron stove really gets going. The old wood-framed chimneys were not designed to stand that much heat. Remember the fate of the old Thompson house that was destroyed by fire in 1984.

This brings us to the subject of whether our old house is unique. We have not heard of any other old house—or new for that matter—still in use that has no modern conveniences or

Photo by Davyd Hood
The shower house

*Spring water flows into the stainless steel tank that
Richard Colgan installed in 1983.*

Our grandchildren, Matthew and Oliver Lewis, waiting for the water to heat in the shower house, 1985. Note the kerosene lamp on the wall.

any substitutes. If there is such a house we'd like to hear about it, and we'll step down.

By the 1980s we were using the old house regularly two months a year, March and November, and our children and grandchildren were regular visitors. In addition, we can't count the number of friends who came for meals on our friendly porch in warm weather or around our table in front of the glowing wood stove when it was cold or rainy. Jack put up a sign as you approach the old house. It reads, "Leaving 20th Century/Entering 19th Century."

Jack's sign on the road leading to the old home place

Photo by Jack Hahn
Foundation stones and steps. When our architect daughter, Anne Lewis, saw our old house for the first time, her only comment was, "It isn't built to code."

More and more people heard about the old house and were curious. One man came and asked if he could bring his family to see it. "I want them to see how we lived when I was growing up," he said. "And why we worked so hard to get out of a place like this."

Another man, who came to repair an old table we had bought from Deek Newman, looked at the house and then at us and said, "Are you crazy or what?"

Others who came were less astonished, or at least they refrained from commenting on our sanity. Among our visitors was the younger daughter of John and Sallie Johnson. She is Fannie Johnson Gaynor and lives in nearby Mountain Home, North Carolina. There are many other Johnson heirs, but most

The shed

are descendants of his daughter by his first wife. She was Maggie Johnson Newman, the mother of thirteen children, many of whom had children, so that list is long.

From Johnson's second marriage, only his older daughter, Naomi Johnson Smith, had children, but happily that line is alive and well. She had three sons and today there are many descendants from this line. Of these Corum Smith has been instrumental in keeping the family in touch with us and with their ancestors' old home place. It was he who brought his Aunt Fannie out to see the house. But, alas, she was less than enthusiastic when she saw the shaky old building with its sagging porch.

Nevertheless, word of the old house so authentically preserved spread, and before long we had visitors. School children come with their teachers to experience a slice of Appalachian history. Carlann Osborn of the Saluda School is one of the most enthusiastic such teachers. When her classes come, we persuade Ruby to sit in one of the bedrooms with one of her mother's quilts on the bed, and the children are spellbound and endlessly curious about life way back then. The letters they write beginning, "Dear Miss Ruby" always delight her.

And we have artists who come to sketch and paint, photographers who come to take pictures, and members of historic societies who come to look. In 1994 we were listed on the National Register of Historical Places, and a sign went up proclaiming this honor. It is next to Jack's hand-lettered sign advising visitors that they are entering the nineteenth century.

National Register sign was installed in 1994

It was soon after the National Register sign went up that several newspaper articles with pictures of the old house appeared. As a consequence, several of John and Sallie Johnson's descendants wanted to see the ancestral house. On one such occasion, they brought Aunt Fannie with them for her second visit. By this time she had seen the stories and pictures in the newspapers and knew about the National Register listing. When she arrived, surrounded by a number of her young relatives, I heard her say proudly, "This was my daddy's house."

We were as proud as she was, and as time went on, we had grown to love our mountain home so much that we decided to build a modern house and guest house a quarter mile away. Dictated by advancing age, we needed a house that required less physical energy—indoor plumbing, light at the flick of a switch, and no more wood to chop before breakfast. The new house and guest house are successful with their creature comforts at our command, and yet somehow we seem to have an affinity for the old home place, a yearning from some simpler past. Hardly a day passes without our going there ostensibly "to check it out," but actually it's to experience again and again the nice happy feeling that we get when we enter that wonderful, honest little building, built with love. And loved still.

*Wild flowers in a vase made from an old shoe
found at the old home place*

Photo by Don Wilson

FAMILY TREES

Johnson Family

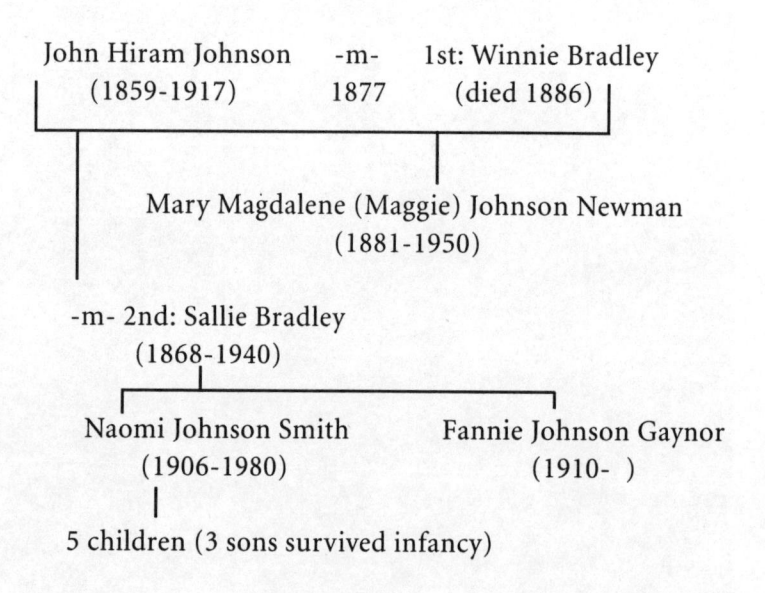

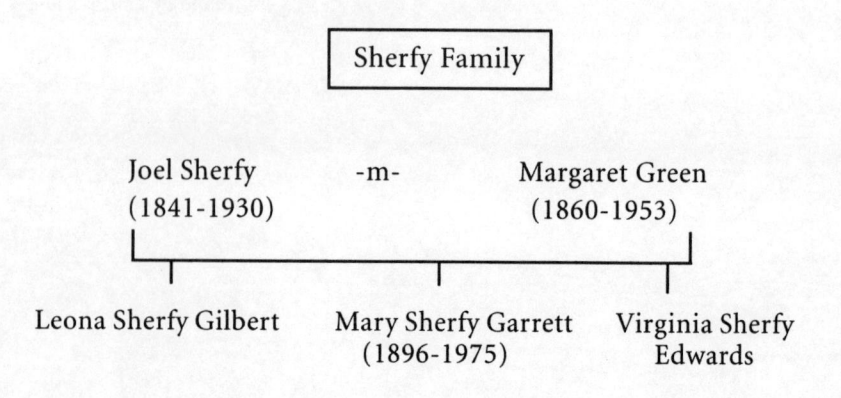

John Hiram Johnson   -m-   1st: Winnie Bradley
(1859-1917)   1877   (died 1886)

Mary Magdalene (Maggie) Johnson Newman
(1881-1950)

-m- 2nd: Sallie Bradley
(1868-1940)

Naomi Johnson Smith   Fannie Johnson Gaynor
(1906-1980)   (1910-)

5 children (3 sons survived infancy)

Sherfy Family

Joel Sherfy   -m-   Margaret Green
(1841-1930)   (1860-1953)

Leona Sherfy Gilbert   Mary Sherfy Garrett   Virginia Sherfy Edwards
(1896-1975)

Garrett Family

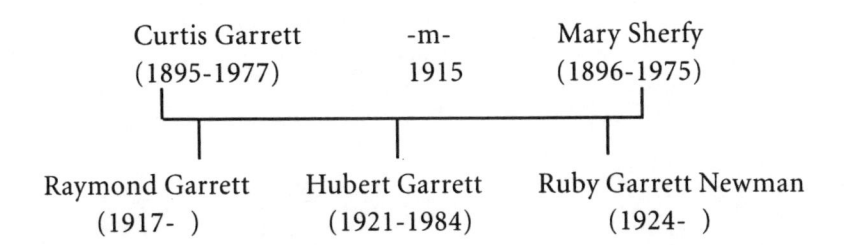

Curtis Garrett   -m-   Mary Sherfy
(1895-1977)   1915   (1896-1975)

Raymond Garrett   Hubert Garrett   Ruby Garrett Newman
(1917-)   (1921-1984)   (1924-)

Newman Family

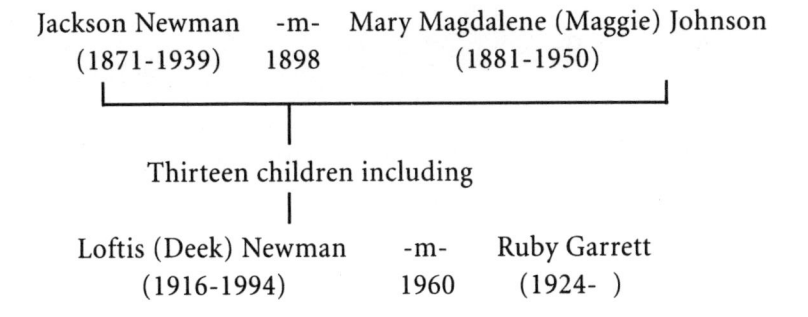

Jackson Newman   -m-   Mary Magdalene (Maggie) Johnson
(1871-1939)   1898   (1881-1950)

Thirteen children including

Loftis (Deek) Newman   -m-   Ruby Garrett
(1916-1994)   1960   (1924-)

Chronology

1729-1788	Gov. William Tryon (governor, 1764-1771)
1855	Polk County achieves county status
1877-1947	Dr. Daniel Lesesne Smith
1878	Railroad comes to Saluda
1881	Saluda (formerly Pace's Gap) chartered and renamed
1887	Old home place built by John H. Johnson
1914	Joel Sherfy buys old home place
1917	Curtis and Mary Sherfy Garrett occupy old home place
1928	Highway 176 completed
1947	First mail delivery on Holbert Cove Road
1954	First electricity on Holbert Cove Road
1966	First telephone service on Holbert Cove Road
1976	Interstate highway I-26 completed
1979	John and Susan Dart McCutcheon buy old home place

ACKNOWLEDGMENTS
and
SOURCES OF INFORMATION

Most of the information about the old home place came from reminiscences of people who once lived there or who went there frequently in the old days. Chief among these were Ruby Garrett Newman and her brother Raymond Garrett; Annie Thompson and her brother Simp Thompson; and their niece Hazel Johnson Jaeger.

Dozens of other people helped by digging up information, lending books, taking pictures, or in the case of Charles O. Hearon Jr. (C.Boy), sketching and painting pictures of the old house as well as reminiscing about the old days. The drawing of the old house is, of course, his.

Others who went out of their way were Tom McHugh, Marvin Alpheus Owings, Corum Smith, and Joseph Wray. Two who went way out of their way were photographers Don Wilson and Jack Hahn. They came out at all hours to get just the right angle in just the right light.

Our three children, Anne Lewis, Mary McCutcheon, and John McCutcheon, encouraged us all the way. Anne drew the floor plan of the old house from Mary's careful measurements, and John has never stopped making improvements.

But above all two people were indispensable: George Jones of Waukegan, Illinois, who did all the computer work for the book (six drafts with maddening additions and corrections in each one), and, of course, my husband, John McCutcheon, who did everything else from feeding the dogs to editing the manuscript.

Susan Dart
Saluda, North Carolina
1997

BOOKS AND PUBLICATIONS

Hearon, Charles O. Jr. *I Remember Saluda, A Storytelling.* Privately published, 1996.

Nodine, Herman. *Sights and Sounds in Saluda.* Privately published, 1993.

Owings, Marvin Alpheus. *Smith Hill, Saluda, North Carolina.* This twenty-nine page family record written in 1995 is bound together with two publications: a 1945 brochure, honoring Dr. Lesesne Smith, and Clara Revenel Smith's 1959 history of the Southern Pediatric Seminar, *The Old Order Changeth.*

Perdue, Theda. *The Cherokee (The Indians of North America* series). New York: Chelsea House Publishers, 1989.

Polk County, North Carolina History. Compiled by the Polk County Historical Association, this 352-page book contains hundreds of photographs, mostly from family albums, and dozens of individual family reminiscences in addition to general anecdotal material about life in Polk County. Published, 1983.

The Saluda Magazine, originally printed from 1936 to 1938. All eight issues were reprinted forty years later as a memorial to Susan Leland Craig, the editor.

Saluda, NC 100 years 1881-1981 (Vol. I & II reprinted 1996) by Anne Osborne and Charlene Pace. Spiral bound, this reissue of the 1981 centennial yearbook consists of over 200 pages of reminiscences and old photos.

A Sense of Heritage, A Pictorial History of the Thermal Belt Area. Sponsored by the Tryon Thermal Belt Chamber of Commerce, this 143-page book is a compilation of anecdotal material with over 100 illustrations. Included is a photograph of the old home place accompanied by an account written by Homar Jones. Published, 1991.

Photo by Don Wilson

Index

A
Asheville, NC, 70

B
Bradley family, 14
Bradley, Sarah (Sallie) (*see* Johnson, Sarah)
Bradley, Winnie (*see* Johnson, Winnie)

C
Cherokee Indians, 11
Chicago Historical Society, 71
Colgan, Richard, 76, 77

E
Edwards, Marvin, 37
electricity, 65, 89

F
Friendship Baptist Church, 20, 30, 37

G
Garrett, Curtis, 37, 43, 48, 50, 54, 59, 65, 89

Garrett family, 66, 70, 87
Garrett, Hubert, 50, 60, 62, 71-72
Garrett, Mary Sherfy, 34, 37-38, 42, 59, 89
Garrett, Mattie (*see* Thompson, Mattie)
Garrett, Molly (*see* Thompson, Molly)
Garrett, Raymond, 43, 50, 60, 91
Garrett, Ruby (*see* Newman, Ruby)
Gaynor, Fannie Johnson, 80, 81, 83
Gilbert, Clifford, 37

H
Hahn, Jack, 91
Hearon, Charles O., 44, 45, 46
Hearon, Charles O. Jr., 27, 46, 91
Henderson County Home, 30
Hendersonville, NC, 76
Highlands, NC, 69
Highway I-26, 89
Highway 176, 89
Holbert Cove [Road], 10, 14, 29, 30, 35, 37, 43, 45, 46, 56, 58, 60, 65, 70, 89
Holbert family, 14

I
Infants' and Children's Sanitarium, 44

J

Jaeger, Hazel Johnson, 56, 91

Johnson, Etta Thompson, 23-25, 54, 56

Johnson family, 66, 86

Johnson, Fannie, 28, 30, 80, 81, 83

Johnson, Gaither, 56

Johnson, Hazel (*see* Jaeger)

Johnson, John Hiram, 9, 10, 14, 19-31, 35, 36, 89

Johnson, Maggie (*see* Newman, Maggie)

Johnson, Naomi, 28, 30, 81

Johnson, Sarah (Sallie) Bradley, 20, 28

Johnson, Winnie Bradley, 19

Jones, George, 91

Jones, Homar, 94

L

Lake Forest-Lake Bluff Historical Society, 72

Lewis, Anne McCutcheon, 68, 80, 91

Lewis, Matthew, 78

Lewis, Oliver, 78

M

mail delivery, 89

McCutcheon, Anne (*see* Lewis)

McCutcheon, Mary, 91

McCutcheon, John III, 91

McCutcheon, John (Jack), 69, 72, 79, 89, 91

McHugh, Tom, 91
McKaig, Katherine, 62
Mt. Lebanon School, 52

N
National Register of Historic Places, 9, 82, 83
Newman, Deek, 60, 61, 62-65, 71, 72
Newman family, 58, 87
Newman, Jack, 25, 28-29, 58
Newman, Maggie Johnson, 19, 20-25, 28, 58, 81
Newman, Ruby Garrett, 50, 56, 57, 61, 62-65, 72, 82, 91
Nodine, Herman, 48, 70
North Carolina, 10, 12, 35, 65, 69
Nostalgia Courtyard, 70

O
Osborn, Carlann, 82
Owings, Marvin Alpheus, 91

P
Pace family, 13
Pace, Herbert, 26
Pace's Gap, 13, 89
Polk, William, 12
Polk County, 10, 12, 36, 89
Prohibition, 46

R
Ricks Haven, 25-28

S
Saluda, NC, 10, 13, 14, 20, 43, 44, 45, 46, 70, 89
Saluda School, 82
Sears Roebuck, 75
Sherfy family, 30-38, 66, 86
Sherfy, Joel, 34, 36-38, 89
Sherfy, Leona, 34, 37
Sherfy, Maggie, 34, 35, 38, 39
Sherfy, Mary (*see* Garrett)
Sherfy, Virginia, 34, 37
Smith, Corum, 81, 91
Smith, D. Lesesne, 44-45, 89
Smith Hill, 46
Smith, Naomi Johnson, 81
Southern Pediatric Seminar, 44, 45
Spartanburg Baby Hospital, 44-45
Spartanburg Herald, 44
stills (distilleries), 46-48
Story, Carl, 28
Story, Jack, 28
Stott, Bobby Joe, 70

T
telephone, 89

Thompson, Annie, 55, 91
Thompson, Etta (*see* Johnson, Etta)
Thompson family, 14, 52, 54, 60
Thompson, Horace, 55-56
Thompson, John, 70
Thompson, Mattie Garrett, 52
Thompson, Molly Garrett, 54
Thompson, Simp, 91
Tryon, NC, 69
Tryon, William, 12, 89

V
Vermont Castings stove, 75

W
Wilson, Don, 91
Wray, Joseph, 91